# Places Via Notes

### Viswaprasad Raju

BookLeaf Publishing
India | USA | UK

Made with ❤ on the BookLeaf Publishing Platform
www.bookleafpub.in
www.bookleafpub.com

# Dedication


"Nobody in Singapore drinks Singapore Slings."

\- Anthony Bourdain

# Preface

Places play

Places pause

Places rewind

Places fast forward

Places don't *stop* to inspire

# Acknowledgements

#TheWriteAngle

# 1. Ameenpur

Ameenpur lake
More a lake system

Home for resident and migratory birds
Lake-front homes for on-site coders and off-shore techies

Built by Ibrahim Qutb shah who ruled the kingdom of
Golconda
Between 1550-1580 AD
A biodiversity heritage site now

# 2. Antarvedi

The beach was his canvas
And every person in and around his aperture
His customer

Competing with tourists chasing sunsets on phone images
He has to show the big picture

His struggle is real
When the tourists film reels

He is on the hunt as the sun is setting
He could convince only one shy couple to picture and print on his Epson printer

He directs them
He knows the spots that make them look good
He is in his element now

The poses are rehearsed
The couple giggle
Standard instructions are doled out
To get stand-out images rolled out

On paper
Not to stay in the gallery of a phone

He looks out at the horizon
With no more customers in sight
Packs his armory
Gets ready to ride away

The lone dog at the beach chases him
Until a distant silhouette is all that remains

# 3. Bandhavgarh

The pitch had some juice in it
Pugmarks
A kill
Alarm calls
But the tiger eluded
Tough luck as Ravi Shastri would put it
Last safari of the trip
The pressure was evident
Call it the slog overs
The last opportunity to score a big one
To hit one out of the park
Inside the national park
In walked the tiger out of the blue
Just like Sir Viv Richards minus the gum though
Same swagger though
He looked around and blended
Into the tapestry of golden yellow
Meadows that glistened in the winter sun
Cameras went click, click, click
Binoculars suddenly became precious property
Everyone congratulated everyone
As if India won the World Cup

# 4. Bhedaghat

Picture this:
Kareena Kapoor at her sensual best
*Raat ka nasha abhi...* from the film Asoka
Reverberates against the gorges
The placid waters of the river Narmada call you
You are in Bhedaghat
Simply marbleous territory
You hear a mighty roar
The visual treat follows not Kareena
The river plunges head on
A cascade of smoke emerges
After the waterfalls
You fall for a boat cruise
After Niagara
It's Grand Canyon
Rocks are no longer only rocks
The guide makes you spot

- An Ambassador car
- An elephant
- A lion's face
- Two kids playing
- A deer
- The horns of a cow

# 5. Cape Town

It took 27 years for Nelson Mandela
For prison break

Ostrich steak to *masala dosa*
Mother city knows how to feed

A riot of colors
A table mountain

# 6. Dubai

A city rises in the middle of a desert

A wetland in a desert

A story of stories in a desert

A Ferrari meets a camel in a desert

# 7. Galle

A poet from Sri Lanka
An author from India
They meet at The Galle Literary Festival

Visit Sri Lanka

The Galle Literary Festival. By the ocean.
It's been making an ocean of difference.
Bringing new writers, new voices to the fore.
Leaving Sinhala and Tamil writers to the folklore.

Visit Sri Lanka

Jaipur Literary Festival.
Galle Literary Festival.
We are always dependent on foreigners to put a spotlight
on our talent.
Even now.

Visit Sri Lanka

Fringed by the indian ocean
Dwarfed by the galle fort

Famed by the sea and sky
Anchored by maritime history
Curated by nature
Crafted for travellers on wanderlust

Visit Sri Lanka

Takes you to Portugal Holland and England
The moment you land

Visit Sri Lanka

Port of call
Stood between the middle east and the orient
A living fort
Stood still for 400 years
Stood to hear many more stories

Visit Sri Lanka

Old buildings are now
Boutiques hotels villas cafes
New buildings now mimic
A bygone era

An UNESCO world heritage site
A site to behold

116 kms from Colombo
Time travel to 400 years and beyond

Visit Sri Lanka

Some upscale resorts here in Galle don't allow either
Indians or Sri Lankans to linger on the private beaches
Both are equally bad according to the resort owners
Equal, once
Andew Fidel Fernando would agree

Visit Sri Lanka

We are a small island
With long names
We are a big country
With complicated names

Visit Sri Lanka

What is in a name?
Tambapanni
Taprobane
Serendip
Tenasserim
Seylan

Ceylon
Lanka
Sri Lanka

Hindoostan
Bharat
India
Bharat

Visit Sri Lanka

You can't miss T in Sri Lanka

T
Tourism
Tigers, once upon a Time
CrickeT
Tsunami
Tears
serendipiTy

And

Black
Green
White
Herbal

Oolong
Hibiscus
Moringa
Cinnamon
Gotukola
Green
Mint
Tea

And
UniTy in diversiTy

Visit Sri Lanka

In both countries
Fair skinned people have an unfair advantage
We are made to believe
It is an insight on which fair and lovely was built
Now it's glow and lovely
Both countries love dark humour
Fair enough

Visit Sri Lanka

Salman Rushdie was a copywriter
Shehan Karunatilaka is a copywriter
They can make the dead alive

Or almost get killed
Based on who you read from the two
With their killer one-liners

Shehan Karunatilaka
Born in Galle
Worked in Amsterdam too
See the Galle Dutch connection

Visit Sri Lanka

Unwelcome visitors
1587 Portuguese
1640 Dutch
1796 English
1980s IPKF
2004 Tsunami

Visit Sri Lanka

War cry
For 30 years
Peace cry
For 30 years

Visit Sri Lanka

Sri Lanka is alien to North Indians
Very much like Pakistan is alien to South Indians

Tremors are not felt when you are far off
Or cut off from neighbouring countries

Visit Sri Lanka

Tropical heat
Cool for many
Hard to beat
Unless you find pockets of air conditioning
At swanky hotels
At cool cafes

Visit Sri Lanka

800
A biopic on Murali
Was to be played by Vijay
The drama unfolded elsewhere
Well played
Well left

Visit Sri Lanka

Indians are going beyond

Kandy
Bentota
Galle

Just like Indians
Sri Lankans are discovering
Jaffna
Pigeon Island
And other equally beautiful parts
War kept these secrets guarded

Visit Sri Lanka
Only South Africa has such a spread as that of Sri Lanka
British
Portuguese
Dutch
Pockets of India as well was a spread

Cricket knows no borders
But it has boundaries

Visit Sri Lanka

Tsunami
A sea of fury
An ocean of anger
A deluge of help

For once
It was not a man made disaster

Visit Sri Lanka

Kill Ravana every year
Hey Ram

Visit Sri Lanka

No lions
No tigers
Only leopards

Visit Sri Lanka

Only when there is
No war
No bomb blasts
No natural disasters
No political circus
No curfew
No this
And no that

Visit Sri Lanka

Sometimes lanka runs on fire
Not on fuel

Visit Sri Lanka

First female prime minister in the world, killed in Sri
Lanka.
First Gandhi to be killed in South India

Visit Sri Lanka

After the end of the war
There was a war of documentaries

Visit Sri Lanka

Small island
Big miracle
How it survived it all
It all
It all

Visit Sri Lanka

Absolute power corrupts
Plunging the country into darkness
Any country

Visit Sri Lanka

Have grown up listening to Ceylon Radio
Have grown up listening to heartbreaking war stories

Visit Sri Lanka

Sri Lankans play rugby with India
Yes
No bonhomie post a game
They think India played a dirty game
Thanks to IPKF
You can't always be a sport
You see

Visit Sri Lanka

At Galle
Some dive from dizzying heights
To earn a few dollars
Even rupees will do
The cost of living is measured
In falling pleasure

Visit Sri Lanka

We come to Lanka for Ramayana Trails
Some come for casinos
Some cum
All are welcome

Visit Sri Lanka

Sigiriya
Sinhala
Tamil
Moors
Christians

Ayodhya?

Visit Sri Lanka

So saffron in 2004
We had to shoot water in Lanka
Instead of Varanasi

So velvet in 2017
We had to shoot Bombay Velvet in Sri Lanka

Visit Sri Lanka

The only sport we sort of excel

Cricket

One world cup each
Played by 12 odd countries

Visit Sri Lanka

We suffer from colonial baggage
We are good at English
We prefer tea and quaint hill station
We crib about their divide-and-rule policy
We continue to follow it though

Visit Sri Lanka

People travel from hill country
To catch waves of sunshine wearing linens
People from the coast travel to hill country
To feel the crisp mountain air wearing sweaters

Visit Sri Lanka

Sri Lankan Frogmouth
Found in India too
Indian Roller
Found in Sri Lanka too
Birds of the same feathers?

Visit Sri Lanka

Our safari jeep drivers are surprisingly well behaved
Our safari jeep drivers aren't
They yell at Yala

Visit Sri Lanka

We have Burghers
We have Parsis

We have Geoffrey Bawa
We have many Bawas
Eight five thousand three hundred ninety seven

Visit Sri Lanka

All our fiction is muddled in
Colonial Baggage
Diaspora Musings

Visit Sri Lanka

China
Chinaman
Both had a great run

In Lanka and beyond

Visit Sri Lanka

The biggest market for Sri Lankan writing in English?
India

Visit Sri Lanka

English writers in Sri Lanka
Are far fewer than the number of books
Inflicted by a certain Chetan
Number speak

Visit Sri Lanka

Kottu roti
Butter chicken
Can't go together
Brilliant
As they are
Separately

Visit Sri Lanka

Our chutneys are their *sambol*
Their hoppers are our *appams*

Visit Sri Lanka

Morning Arrack
English Breakfast
Afternoon Tea
Kottu Roti anytime

Visit Sri Lanka

In India, lotus is blooming
In Sri Lanka lotus tower is shining with Chinese debt

Visit Sri Lanka

Ashoka
The King from India
Came in a chariot
According to legends
Today it would be on an Ashok Leyland

Visit Sri Lanka

Writer Ashok Ferrey
His home is home to many films.
Midnight children
Water

Bombay velvet
He is a celebrity trainer
You figure

Visit Sri Lanka

Muttiah Muralitharan
800th
Shane Warne
500th

Rebuilt from scratch
When Warne and Murali came together
Built on the foundation of hope
After the tsunami rage

Visit Sri Lanka

The Dutch Reformed Church
Of gravestones
Of carved letters and motifs
Of a Dutch Commander
Of a long awaited daughter
of Dutch Ceylon
of suspended time

Visit Sri Lanka

An UNESCO world heritage site
A site to behold
116 kms from Colombo
time travel to 400 years and beyond

Visit Sri Lanka

Carry masks
Made by the local artisans
Mask that unmasks many stories
Carry home memories

Visit Sri Lanka

The Family Man
The Night Manager
They are not the same
both were shot in Sri Lanka though

Visit Sri Lanka

India RRR
Sri Lanka
Remarkable
Relentless
Resplendent

Visit Sri Lanka

27

Mani Ratnam directed Kannathil Muthamittal
Mani Ratnam co-produced Paradise
Beautiful Place?

Visit Sri Lanka

We read
We write
While our worlds burn
Outside
We burn
Inside


Visit Sri Lanka

# 8. Goa

**Mario Miranda's Goa**
**Remo Fernandes' Goa**
**Kishori Amonkar's Goa**
**Ileana D'Cruz's Goa**
**Wendell Rodricks' Goa**
**Damodar Mauzo's Goa**
**Maria Aurora Couto's Goa**

**Everyone's Goa**

# 9. Hampi

Dream-like
Surreal
Real
Dream

Romance the stones
Delve into history
See the river Tungabhadra glide past
Sway under a mango tree
Do a coracle ride
Do nothing

Switch between browns and greens
Between rocks and ruins
Between time and timelessness

# 10. Jim Corbett Tiger Reserve

Of *The land of roar trumpet and song*
Of *Carpet Sahib*
Of *Jungle Lore*
Of *My India*
Of *The Man eaters of Kumaon*
Of *The temple tiger and more man eaters of Kumaon*
Of *The hunter's friends*
Of *The man eating leopard of Rudraprayag*
Of India's first national park
Of Jim Corbett via his books

# 11. Kerala

Achingly lush
Calmingly quiet
Nothing comes hurtling at you
You set the pace
Backwater houseboat speed
Languid
Slow
Gentle
Calm
You flow
With the current
Not against it

# 12. Kolkata

Adda
Bata
China town
Dada
East India Company
Football
Ghugni chaat
Hooghly
Illissh
Joy
Kati roll
Lal paar saree
Maidan
Nobel prize winners
O 'Kolkata
Pandals
Quest mall
Ray
Sweets
Tagore
Usha Uthap
Vintage trams
Writer's building

X' mas celebrations
Yellow taxis
Zoo

# 13. Ladakh

Raw & Fragile
Remember to breathe & Breathtaking
Thukpa & Apricot Jam
Hemis National Park & Night Sky Sanctuary
Monasteries & Stupas
Union & Territory
Prayer flags & High passes
Otherworldly & Inner-worldly

# 14. London-Hyderabad

City of River Thames
City of River Musi

City of hunting grounds turned into Royal Parks
City of hunting grounds turned into National Parks

City of Downing Street, SW1
City of 10 Downing Street, Begumpet

City of Hunting Grounds turned into Royal Parks
City of Hunting Grounds turned into National Parks

City of Fish & Chips
City of Fish Cooperative Building

City of Big Ben
City of Charminar

City of Columbia Road Flower Market
City of Gudimalkapur Flower Market

City of High-gate Cemetery
City of Qutub Shahi Tombs

City of Bahubali at Royal Albert Hall
City of Bahubali at Ramoji Film City

City of Queen's Park
City of Begumpet

City of St. Paul's Cathedral
City of St. John's The Baptist Church

City of the British
City of We Faithful, ally of the British Government

City of Portland Stone
City of Lime Mortar and Granite

City of Shakespeare
City of Pirs

City of Truefitt & Hill, since 1805
City of Truefitt & Hill, since 2021

City of Once the richest city in history
City of Home of the richest Indian in history

City of Dreams
City of Palaces

City of Much Ado About Nothing
City of *Light Lo Yaaron*

City of Bluebells
City of Golden Blooms

City of Brown Whites
City of White Mughals

City of The Great Exhibition in 1851
City of Numaish Exhibition, since 1938

City of Black Cab
City of Yellow Auto

City of Lord's
City of Nawabs

City of London Greys
City of Hyderabad Blues

City of Greater London Authority
City of Hyderabad Metropolitan Development Authority

City of Kew Gardens
City of Botanical Gardens

City of Primrose Hill
City of Banjara Hills, Jubilee Hills etc

City of Hyde (park)
City of Public (gardens)

City of Salar Jung Memorial Hall
City of Salar Jung Museum

City of Foodies' Heaven
City of Foodies' Paradise

City of Queue
City of *Kyun*

City of King's Cross
City of 'X' Roads

City of Strawberry
City of Baingan

City of Double-deckers
City of Double-deckers

City of Houses of Parliament
City of New Secretariat

City of The Great Fire of London in 1666
City of The Great Musi Flood of 1908

City of no-return gifts
City of a gift to Queen Elizabeth II a matching tiara and a
diamond platinum necklace as a wedding present

City of British Museum
City of Salar Jung Museum

City of London Plane Tree
City of Gulmohar

City of The Al Saqi books closing its doors after 44 years
City of The A A Hussain and Co closing after 65 years

City of Speaker's Corner, Hyde Park
City of Lamakaan, near Dr Vengal Rao Park

City of St. Paul's
City of HPS

City of MCC (Marylebone Cricket Club), founded in 1787
City of HCC (Hyderabad Cricket Club), founded in 1931

City of Wimbledon
City of Sania Mirza

City of Cricket
City of Kirkit

City of Cadbury's
City of Nizam's Sugars

City of BAT (British American Tobacco)
City of VST (Vazir Sultan Tobacco)

City of Only Dunhill will do.
City of Relax. Have a Charminar.

City of Theatre
City of Cinema

City of Fazl Mosque
City of Mecca Masjid

City of Baron Bilimoria
City of Karan Bilimoria

City of Maison Bertaux, since 1871
City of Karachi Bakery, since 1953

City of Oyster Card
City of Pearls

City of Liverpool (Station)
City of Lakdi-ka-pool (Station)

City of Jubilee Line
City of Jubilee Hills

City of Literature
City of Bards

City of Raymond Williams
City of Michel Joachim Marie Raymond

City of The Shaftesbury Memorial Fountain
City of Gulzar Houz

City of Blue Plaque
City of Blue Sea

City of British Airways
City of The Deccan Airways

City of Camden Market
City of Moazzam Jahi Market

City of London Transport Museum
City of Sudha Cars

City of Royal Observatory
City of Birla Planetarium

City of Kohinoor
City of Kohinoor

City of Taj Buckingham 51 suites
City of Taj Falaknuma

City of Londinium, London
City of Bhagyanagar, Hyderabad

City of Romans Anglo, Saxons, Vikings, Normans
City of Qutub Shahis, Mughals, Asif Jahis

City of afternoon tea
City of anytime chai

City of Hyde Park
City of Public Gardens

City of Tower Bridge
City of Cable Bridge

City of Jellied Eels Pie Mash
City of Biryani Lukmi Haleem

City of Greenwich Mean Time
City of Hyderabadi Standard Time

City of the Buckingham Palace
City of Chowmahalla Palace

City of seen 3000 summers Totteridge Yew
City of 400 year old Hatiyan Jhad Baobab Tree

City of 3000 plus parks
City of 1000 plus parks

City of urban foxes
City of Fox Sagar

City of doves & pigeons
City of doves & pigeons

# 15. Mauritius

Copy Mauritius
Paste heaven
Said someone today

Broadly three sets of travellers
Migrants
Pilgrims
Honeymooners
Said a travel agent the other day

Grand Basin
Chamarel Islands
Seven coloured earth
Deer island
Caudan waterfront
Pamplemousses botanical garden
Said the guide every day

# 16. Mumbai

45

157 sq km
30,85,411 people
35 leopards
26/11
6 sigma dabbawalas
7 islets
1 bollywood

Mombayn
Bombay
Bombain
Bombaym
Monbaym
Mombaim
Mombaym
Bambaye
Bombaiim
Bombeye
Boon bay
Bon bahia
Mumbai

# 17. Perupalem

A battery of quacking ducks took over the road
Enroute
A stream of cutouts of Telugu heroes
Enroute

You smell salt soon
You sight temples and churches
You get pushed and pulled by the rhythmic dance of
waves
You stand to float
You float to stand

Young couples steal glances
Hungry crows attempt to steal food

A pod of dolphins afar
You listen to music via ear-pods

# 18. Pillalamarri

A date with a 700-year-old tree
A lot can happen under a tree, especially if it's a banyan
tree
A tree of immortality

In literature, Robinson Crusoe built his home on one
R K Narayan wrote Under the banyan tree and other
stories
In Gujarat it sheltered Alexander's army of 7000

Am at Pillalamarri
It is older than Amsterdam
Spread over 3 acres
Among the eight great Indian banyan trees
More a forest in itself than a tree
The canopy spread is beguiling
You can't figure out the roots from the branches
The mother trunk from its far-flung siblings
Out here a morning or an evening walk
Means just a walk around the tree

# 19. Switzerland

Not all are cold bankers
Or bearded farmers

Some you will be fond-ue of
Muesli you won't know them

Albert Einstein
Carl Gustav Jung
Henri Nestlé
H R Giger
Roger Federer
Ursula Andress

# 20. Tadoba

Mountain people
Beach people
There are also wildlife people

They thrive in no network places
They are one with nature
They buffer
They core
They machan
They gypsy
They wait for that one moment
They click
They film
They observe
They document
They sing bird songs
They are lost
They are found
They drift
They woods

# 21. West Wycombe

Palladian
Neoclassical

*Fast & Furious* was filmed here
So was *Sense & Sensibility*

Home of the Dashwood family for over 300 years
Open for wedding events these days

A pleasure palace
Known for cave parties
Some of the elite club members:
William Hogarth
John Wilkes
Thomas Potter
John Montagu
Benjamin Franklin

Eight rooms
The hall
The dining room
The tapestry room
The yellow saloon

The red drawing room
The study
The blue drawing room
The music room

Painted ceilings
Ornate fireplaces
Family heirlooms
Portraits
Chandeliers
Classical busts
Tapestries
Many secrets

www.ingramcontent.com/pod-product-compliance
Lightning Source LLC
LaVergne TN
LVHW050935200726
843508LV00011B/2348